Through My Eyes

Through My Eyes

Mechael Hayes

ISBN: 0692748598
ISBN 13: 9780692748596
Library of Congress Control Number: 2016910755
De'Angelo Hayes, Mount Vernon, IL

Contents

CHAPTER 1

Thinking Back

I SIT STARING OUT THE window; I never really have been one to sleep much. It's the middle of the night as I sit and think about where I am today and what my aspirations for the future are. My body is riddled with reminders of where I have been, the past I have been running away from, and the price one can pay for the simple luxuries most people take for granted. I spend my day trying to heal wounds and accomplish goals while living as close to societal standards and what the world considers normal. The ability to lay my head down without worrying about who's looking for me or always being on alert and ready to harm people before they get me is a very settling feeling. Yet the fear of letting my guard down even for a moment keeps me at a very high level of anxiety.

My new life has taken some time to get used to. I hurt a lot of people in my life with my inability to love or connect to anyone. There is an unimaginable cold that has lingered in my heart for a very long time. Most days I feel like a walking zombie, with no direction in life. There are a lot of people who have left my life and whom I wish I could have back or could have at least apologized to.

I began writing as a form of therapy, trying to put the demons of my past behind me. Then the realization that there are many others out there with stories similar to mine fueled my passion to finish writing my story, to show others that even though all scars don't heal, and we can't always forget the bad things that happen to us, we can still have a happy and fulfilling life.

I was watching a movie on friendships and relationships when I realized I've never allowed anyone to get close to me. I began to think back on all the people I hurt, and I became filled with sorrow. I believe people are responsible for their own actions, but I also believe environment influences behavior—especially during childhood. I hope my story helps others from backgrounds similar to mine to never let the things they have been through define them. Allowing the things others do to us to burden our lives gives others control of us. We can take our power back.

CHAPTER 2

The Beginning

FROM A VERY YOUNG AGE, I felt there had to be more to life for me than I saw immediately around me. My mother had odd taste in men. The trait they all shared was that they loved to hit women. My mother had me when she was very young and didn't seem to have a natural maternal instinct for parenting. I never had the chance to develop that mother-child bond that most children have. My great-grandparents were my caregivers when I was young; although my father lived on the same street as me when I was a child, he was completely absent from my life.

I was raised in the city of Detroit. Detroit during the early '90s wasn't much different than the city is today. Each street was half occupied, and for every house that was occupied, there were the remains of an abandoned home. Jobs were few, and as in any underfunded, underdeveloped area, crime was rampant. The streets were littered with debris and smelled of gun smoke and urine. It was a city where you were forced to grow up quickly.

Dead bodies were the norm. My first encounter with a dead body was when I was a small child, around five or six years old. I was walking through an alley with my friend when we came across a body of a young woman who had been killed. She was a young, attractive white woman who was completely nude. We poked her skin with a stick. I tried to fondle her breast like I had seen on television but was utterly disappointed, as they were cold and hard. We soon grew bored and continued on with our day. We were so desensitized by our environment that we never thought to tell anyone about it.

I grew up in my grandparents' home. Both were good people in their own ways. They were both drunks, and each of them handled that in his or her own way with his or her own manners and temperaments. My great-grandfather George was a giant of a man, with a great heart. I have no memories of him ever raising his voice or his hand at me. We always started our days off bright and early with a cup of coffee as soon the sun was rising. He was one of my favorite people in the entire world. A lot of who I am today is because of him.

My great-grandmother was the opposite. Her attitude toward everyone, mixed with her alcohol-dependency problem, made a very bad combination. It was from her that my hateful and distorted views on life and women began to fester. I always knew she loved me; she just had her own special way of showing me. She had an anger with the world that I could never quite figure out, and I didn't have guts to ask her about it.

I learned how to handle myself at a very young age. I once got into an argument with my childhood friend during which he slit my arm open with a knife. I went home with my pride hurt while feeling I had lost the fight. I arrived home with my flesh torn and blood pouring out of my arm. My childhood puppy-love girlfriend, Tatianna, escorted me home. I thought I had a decent lie to tell my great-grandmother so she wouldn't know I had been fighting or that I had lost. Unbeknown to me, an adult had witnessed the whole thing and phoned ahead. Once I arrived home, Big Mamma was there to greet me. "What happened?" she asked.

"I fell!" I replied, deciding on that lie to hide my shame.

She slapped me so hard across the face that my ears were ringing and my cheek was on fire. After I realized she already knew the truth, I told her the whole story. Before I could get my last few words out, she began to slap me repeatedly and throw me around the porch—all while my arm continued to bleed, by the way. She informed me that one of the reasons for the beating was because I was a tattletale for telling her what the kid did to me, which confused me more, considering I was hit the first time for not telling her exactly what happened to me. She also berated me for losing the fight. After beating me even worse than I had been beaten in the fight, she threw a tube of Neosporin at me and said, "Men take care of themselves."

For a while after that, I sat crying and crying, still holding on to that little shred of hope that I might be consoled. That was the exact moment I began to realize I was on my own. This epiphany had lasting effects on me. Living in that house turned me to stone, through and through, at a very young age. I learned to be very clever and defend myself rather well. I learned to conceal my misdeeds.

There came a time in my mother's life when she finally decided she would actually try to be a mother. She packed me and my brother up and moved us to Evanston, Illinois. I don't really remember the trip to Illinois, although I vaguely remember my uncle John driving us. I do remember staying in a hotel a couple of nights, pretending to be asleep while having to listen to my mother and her friend having sex. We moved into a new apartment, and for awhile things really did begin to get better. My mother, little brother, and I had a small one-bedroom apartment in Evanston. We were happy for the first time I could ever remember, being with my mother. I was going to a nice school, and I excelled with my peers and in academics. This was the last moment I remember truly being happy, and never will I forget the day all that changed.

There was a knock at the door; my mother answered, and a man entered. He was dark as night and built like a monster. I knew even at my young age that things were about to change, but I never would have guessed how much. Phil was an old boyfriend of my mother's who came straight to our house after being released from prison. He was a very controlling man who had no patience for children and a very short temper. It didn't take long for our short, joy-filled life to come crashing down.

My first of many painful and vivid memories is that of an incident that happened shortly after he moved in. I was in first or second grade, and school had just ended for the day. We lived over a mile away from the school. As I was walking home, I saw a black two-door vehicle just up ahead with a young man inside it. He opened the passenger door and began to speak to me, urging me to come over to the car. He unbuckled his seat belt as if he were preparing to strike if needed. I slowly began to walk toward the open door knowing what would happen to me if I did not come up with an escape plan quickly. (Growing up in my home town gave me a great deal of street smarts, even though I was young.) Once I was about five feet from the car, however, I started running in the opposite direction. I ran faster than ever before, with the only thought in my head being to make it home safely.

I burst into the house, but before I could get a word out about the terrifying encounter, I caught an open hand to the face. Before I could catch my breath or tell my family what happened, as I stood there panting and out of breath, Phil began to scream at me once again. I started to speak and was told not to interrupt him, and then I was yelled at again. My punishment for making it home that fast was having to make that timing every day getting home from school from then on—with the threat of being beaten if I did not. I never did get to tell them what horrific thing I had gone through just minutes before. I decided then that it wouldn't have mattered either way.

CHAPTER 3

Struggling to Adjust

⁓

VIOLENCE BECAME THE NORM TO me. I began to expect it—to the point that I no longer feared its arrival. I was out with my auntie, and the house we were in was invaded by two men with guns. They made us all get on the floor. I remember one of them pointing the gun at the back of my head and threatening to kill me if the adults didn't give him whatever it was that he was looking for. I had had enough near-death experiences by my eighth birthday that I was just numb to them.

The abuse at home began to happen more frequently, growing in brutality as time went on. My hatred for Phil and his for me began to fester over time. The emotional and mental abuse became a daily routine, as well as the beatings. My grades began to slip. I started getting into altercations at school. This is where my lying began, with daily excuses for my multiple bruises. My brother, for reasons beyond me, was pardoned from all forms of abuse. If he did anything wrong, I took the fall for it. I wasn't allowed to play sports or have friends or even engage in extracurricular activities. I began to get into trouble at school so that I would have to stay over in detention, giving me time away from home. My viewpoint was that I was going to be beaten either way, so I might as well delay it as much as possible.

One extracurricular activity that Phil forced upon me was stealing. Money was scarce, and there wasn't much to go around. Stealing him beers became a daily routine. It was early in the morning one day, and Phil didn't feel like watching my little brother, so Phil made me bring Jeremiah with me. You can pretty much guess what happened next: I was caught for stealing. Phil beat me pretty badly that morning. I bled from everywhere, and he made sure to inform me that the beating was not for the crime but actually for getting caught.

I really began to build up a thicker skin after that beating, but just as I began to adapt, so did he. New and much crueler tactics became part of the beatings. He began to implement rigorous workouts. After each and every beating, he would force me to get into squatting position with my hands out in front of me. Once while I was bleeding and drained from the beating I had received, he forced me to assume this position and stay that way for twelve hours. This number is not an exaggeration. Phil, my mother, and also my little brother took turns watching me; I was trembling, shaking, and fighting the constant urge to fall from the never-ending pain and buckling of my knees. If my form or posture began to falter, I was struck forcefully by Phil but told not to move. Losing my balance and falling meant starting all over again. With hatred and amazement, I watched my mother and brother, who were quite easily able to ignore my pain and abuse.

When I was around thirteen years old, Phil said he believed I was old enough to start pitching in. He made it very clear that he had no interest in how I earned money, as long as it was coming in. Panhandlers, a pizza parlor within walking distance of our house, needed help and hired me on the spot. I still thank God for that because my fear of him would have made me do just about anything to bring home money. I worked after school and on days off. I loved that job; it meant the world to me. I was only thirteen years old, but because of the desperation on my face, the owner didn't ask me any questions.

My main reason for loving the job was that it kept me out of the house and away from the beatings. From my first paycheck, Phil started taking my money for the weekly rent he said I had to pay, since I lived there and was able to take care of myself and pitch in. After he was done taking rent, there wasn't anything left. I thought I was clever one week; I cashed my paycheck and bought myself a couple of items. I was halfway through my shift when he stormed in and proceeded to drag me out to the car. Once we were inside the vehicle, he began to repeatedly punch me in my face. I was told I was no longer going to be working there. Once he said that, my world came crashing down; my workplace had been my only escape from the hell that was waiting for me every second at home.

The severity of his beatings was based on his mood in that moment. On some rare occasions, he didn't just use his feet and fist; he also used cable cords, phone cords, or anything that could inflict the severest pain. I can't remember the number of times I could barely move because I was so covered in welts and bruises. To this day I am covered from head to toe in scars as reminders of what I went through in that house.

One day I came home from running another one of his errands. As soon as I entered the door, he grabbed me around the throat, picked me up, and slammed me on the ground; then he began to repeatedly stomp me on my face. I was in a state of semiconsciousness, and it felt like every other kick was pushing me more toward unconsciousness. He picked me up, wrapped his hand around my throat, and, with one hand, pinned me against the wall, my feet dangling off the ground. With his other hand, he repeatedly slapped and punched me over and over. I just took the beating; I didn't make a sound. When he saw that I couldn't take anymore and that I was about to break, he threw me to the ground. I didn't have the strength to get up, so I was forced to half crawl and half scurry to my room. I was in too much pain to sleep, so I just sat in the corner.

I was relieved it was over, but sadly the relief was short lived. After giving me about an hour to recuperate, he sent my little brother in to get me. It was the first week of summer, and I was informed that I would be spending my entire summer inside my room. I wasn't allowed to eat with my family, and I wasn't allowed out of my room. I was so terrified of being beaten that I started limiting my trips to the restroom. I didn't realize that I was slowly being turned into an animal in the most primitive sense. I began urinating in the corners of my room as if I was an animal; it became second nature to me—anything to keep me from leaving the room and getting beaten.

I resorted to waiting till everyone in the house had fallen asleep and eating raw meat and raw eggs because Phil wouldn't allow me to eat very often. Being alone and secluded for such long durations, I learned to mask my true self behind a shell I created for protection. I have always been amazed at how much trauma and abuse the human body can sustain and still keep going. As I began to realize how brutal my abuse was, I also realized my purity and innocence were gone, and a cold, loveless empty shell took their place.

CHAPTER 4

Unbreakable

—ↄ

THE YEARS OF PAIN AND abuse found a way to numb my body and in some instances actually bring me pleasure. One evening after a long day of drinking, Phil called me into the living room where he was drinking with a friend. He then took the shade off the floor lamp next to us and stuck the bulb, which had been on for a large part of the day, onto my bare chest. As the hot bulb burned into my chest, I could smell my flesh burning. When the skin burned away, I began to bleed; after a couple of minutes had passed, the bulb popped—I assume from being smeared with my blood. I could always see his hatred for me, but the look on his face in that moment had more hatred than I had ever seen. I hadn't even made a sound the entire time I was going through this, and I believe he took that as an insult. Yet I was happy because in that moment, I knew that no one could ever hurt me again.

The beatings escalated and became even more frequent after that day. My body was unbreakable, but I began to fall emotionally and mentally into a deep abyss. Still shackled by the pain and fear that had been embedded in me over the years, I began to feel a lot of hatred for myself. With every day that passed, I could feel my fear being replaced with hatred more and more.

One morning Phil and I were the only two home, and I had just gotten out of the shower. I was wearing only a towel, and as I bent down to grab my shirt, he reached out and grabbed my backside. This was the first time I remember telling myself that I was willing to die before I let that go any further. He saw that I wasn't willing to let that happen, and he walked away. Later that afternoon he grabbed me around my throat and lifted me into the air. While I stared into his eyes, he proceeded to bang my head against the wall. As he squeezed tighter, like a vise grip, I began to get dizzy; my head felt as if it were going to pop off. The second before I was on the verge of blacking out, he threw me to the ground. I came to when my feet made contact with the ground. He then proceeded to kick me in the face over and over again.

Never once, during all the different forms of abuse that I received, did I ever shed a tear in front of him. I have always taken pride in that.

My depression reached its worst point ever. Thoughts of suicide filled my mind. I had become unbreakable, unbeatable, and able to take anything. My own worst nightmare had become myself. I became evil in every sense of the word. I didn't care about anything or anyone. I never learned what it meant to love someone. I never knew how to be loved or to accept love. I knew how to use and abuse and inflict pain on the people I should have loved. This was all I knew, all I saw, and all I had been put through. This man filled my childhood with pain and abuse during some of the most important developmental stages of my youth. Because of the abuse, I never learned the ability to love or mourn.

CHAPTER 5
Hatred

⟿

BEFORE PHIL WAS IN THE picture, I was a mama's boy. By the time high school started, I hated my mother. For years, she watched firsthand the abuse I received. When he would beat me so badly that I was covered with bruises and gashes and was gushing blood, I would wait in my room for her to come in and save me or at least console me. That day never came. I would beg and cry for us to leave. She just kept telling how much she needed him. He would beat me to a pulp, throw me in a room, and make me go days without food. My body is a detailed canvas reflecting the acts of his hatred for me.

CHAPTER 6

Praying to God

MY LITTLE BROTHER WAS SPARED from all of this for some reason. I would receive a beating for anything he did, even when I wasn't around him. He took advantage of that very often. Because he saw all the things that I was going through, my brother saw me as less than him. I felt I was in a house full of strangers whom I hated with a passion. I hated them but felt a loyalty to my mom and my brother because we were blood. I would lie down at night and pray to die.

One night I thought I had received my wish. My brother and I had an argument, and he lunged at me with a pocket-knife. The knife struck me right below my kneecap. It was the middle of the night, and we were the only two awake. He immediately began to feel remorse. Blood was pouring out of my leg, and I grew very light-headed. Instead of panicking, I was relieved and happy. Blood was pouring out pretty fast, so I calmed my brother down, told him to go to bed, and went to the bathroom. I ran some bathwater and then lay in the tub. I closed my eyes and left the rest in God's hands.

Some people fear death; I feared life. Some days I begged for death to come for me. Some days I loved God; on others I hated him. I couldn't understand why he felt I deserved that pain or what I could have done that was so bad; I was still only a child.

I tried every way I could think of to kill myself. Nothing worked. I never cut deeply enough or took enough pills to do more than get sick. I felt God wanted me to go through this, but I didn't understand why. I just wanted a normal childhood. That wasn't in the cards for me.

That night, in the bathtub, I could feel the blood loss taking effect; I began to drift away. Phil woke up in the middle of the night to use the restroom. He found me lying in the water, which had become bright red. I remember him asking, "What did you do?" He grabbed me out of the tub to take me to the hospital.

By this point, after being unable to find an escape, I felt so alone. My father was never in the picture; my mother and brother watched me being beaten, punched, kicked, slapped, thrown around, and treated as nothing for years. I felt I had no one to turn to and that I was on my own. My heart became stone, incapable of felling. My mother's inability to love me, her son, enough to save me caused me to inadvertently have a mistrust and deep-rooted hatred of women. I lusted for their bodies but was incapable of much more. My mother had caused me to feel all women were coldhearted, loveless, soulless beings that couldn't be trusted. I never took the time to reflect on what was done to me. I wasn't allowed to be around anyone else or to build healthy relationships or friendships. So I had to assume that everyone was this way. This was the only life I knew.

CHAPTER 7

Escaping

‿ↄ

My freshman year of high school was vague and unimportant. I hadn't begun to come into my own yet, still shackled by the fear Phil had instilled in me over the years. I thought things were beginning to look up in some ways; he told me I could try out for the football team. After I made the team and came home to tell him, however, he told me he had changed his mind and that I couldn't play. He knew football was my dream.

This is when my lying to my friends and classmates started. I had to lie about why I couldn't play with my classmates and make up reasons for why I couldn't hang out or be a normal adolescent. It also damaged a lot of my relationships with people at school.

I was allowed to have small dates with a girl named Donchelle. She was a senior while I was a freshman. I was shy and very naïve, but she was the sweetest girl I had ever met. I was still a virgin, so just being around her made me happy. But after each date, I was severely beaten. She was the first girl I ever dated, and she really liked me, so I took those beatings because a couple of hours here and there with her were my only short escape. Eventually, though, as with everything else good in my life, Phil found a way to destroy that as well by not allowing me to continue my relationship with Donchelle.

Lying had become second nature to me. I had to lie to doctors about scars, to teachers about why I missed school and why I wasn't focused, and to friends on a daily basis. I lied about what I was going through because I didn't want anyone's pity.

We moved again after freshman year. Phil was never good with finances, so we moved a lot. During the summer before sophomore year, I began to come out of my fear. I realized that all the thousands of beatings, countless instances of verbal abuse, hours of torturous military-style discipline regimens, starvation, and everything else made me see that he hadn't broken me and couldn't—or at least I hadn't been broken.

I lost my virginity that summer. I had multiple female friends who tried before that, but I was too scared. It was a week before school. I had no idea what I was doing. I had been locked away for months at a time, with no human contact or television and no one to talk to but myself. I spent so much time confined that the stories and people I made up in my head were more real to me than a person standing in front of me. I had no life experience in anything. Because of the religion my mother and Phil practiced, I had never celebrated a single holiday or birthday. I was a nobody with nothing to tell about myself because I didn't know myself. The only good memory I had of my years at home was my first orgasm. I became obsessed with sex and masturbated multiple times a day. I had no real connection to any human being.

One night I was reading a book, and I remember just thinking that life outside of here couldn't be much worse, so I ran away that night and never looked back. I thought I was escaping my hell. The environment I was forced to go through, however, left me ill prepared for life on the streets. I spent a year homeless while still in high school, eating out of garbage cans and wearing the same two outfits for weeks at a time. Phil's beatings and abuse made me strong. I had to do horrible things to survive. But I survived, and now, ten years later, I'm just starting to build the life I want for myself and my family. I am not proud by any means for a lot of the things I have done in my life. I may not be where I want to be, but I'm progressing. It takes time and work to try to heal wounds.

CHAPTER 8
Life

I DIDN'T WRITE THIS SHORT story of my life for sympathy, fame, or anything like that. I wrote this because I know there are millions of people out there going through their own personal forms of hell. We can't control a lot of the situations we are faced with or many of the different forms of abuse that come our way. The same abuse applied to two different people can give two very different outcomes. Abuse can cause one person to become a serial killer and another to become a counselor.

Depression, lack of ambition, and low self-esteem are just a few of the symptoms and signs of abuse. Millions of people, children and adults alike, battle with the effects of an abusive life. I left home, and for some time afterward, I was extremely shy and afraid of everything. My confidence was nonexistent. I had spent my entire childhood being told I was worth nothing, and I had come to believe it. My mother's husband had forced me to be his personal slave. I cleaned every room until it was spotless, no matter who made the mess. Something so mundane may not seem very traumatic to some, but for me it was as traumatic as the rest of the abuse. I spent hours each day on my hands and knees, scrubbing toilets and watching everyone else have fun while I was forced to be the maid at his beck and call. To this day I battle with OCD, trying to control the urge to have everything perfect.

We will all face some form of resistance and obstacles in our lives. Some troubles are unavoidable, but never let anyone make you believe your worth is less than you deserve.

The term "moderation" didn't have much meaning for me until I began to reflect upon and conquer the effects my abuse had on me. I fought depression, self-hatred, and the general feeling of worthlessness by building an inner reserve of strength. I couldn't tell anyone about the things I was going through while I was living under that roof. Fear of speaking up about the abuse consumed me. I didn't think anyone would believe me, and I was afraid that speaking up would end in dire consequences for me. I had to train my mind to become a warrior. I never developed the ability to love or to be loved. Having your childhood spent with your mother allowing a man to use you as his personal punching bag and being a victim of various forms of abuse changes you as a person and most times not for the better. I lost my best friend and one of the greatest women to grace my life because I could not speak up regarding my abuse. Anger and pain were the only emotions that I understood or knew how to express. There was no crying when a family member died and no mourning for friends; I just didn't know how to care. Hugs, affection,

and even kisses made me uncomfortable. The more someone showed me love, the more uncomfortable I began to feel
around them. Love was a quality I was never shown, so I
did not know how to respond to or appreciate it. Lying had
become my best friend; I had to lie so much to hide my pain
and my shame that by the time I realized how many lies I had
told to bury my abuse, it would be like rewriting history by
telling the truth.

The only quality worth mentioning that I possessed during my teenage years was protector. I battled my entire youth
with wanting to die because of how numb I had become from
the things that I had gone through and because of my inability to love in a normal way or tell my story. When I did have
something that meant the world to me, I dug in. My girlfriend Jasmine was in her car with her baby sister when some
guy tried to open her car door and grab her. I remember that
when she called me crying, all rational and normal thoughts
left my mind. I walked that area for hours, questioning people and looking for this person. I'm actually glad I didn't find
him, because my intent was to take a life that day. Protection
was the only trait I correlated with love, and people in my life
knew I was willing to cross any line to keep them safe, so they
never worried.

Some people are just intent on trying to hurt you and
bring you down. I finally got the courage to run away, and I
never looked back. This act of defiance must have infuriated
Phil, because shortly thereafter my longtime girlfriend and
her mother received a visit from him and my mother. They

proceeded to tell them how bad a person I was. It was his way of doing whatever he could to show me he could still take what mattered most to me.

Strength can be a blessing and a curse. I have lost almost everything a person could lose. My inability to feel made me a walking zombie. I started doing drugs, became violent, and was very promiscuous. Sex was my only escape from my demons. It was my drug, and I needed that constant high. My life became a collection of failed relationships, fake friends, and sleepless nights. I have made a lot of bad choices and carry many regrets. I committed some sins that I will have to carry to my grave, only confessing them to God.

"A Note to Fellow Victims." For those who are coming from similar or worse circumstances, I want you to know you can be and have what you want. I continue to live with the scars of my past, and I don't know if I'll ever fully recover. But for my own sake, I have to try. And for those of you who are lucky enough to have a normal and stable upbringing with loving parents, I want you to see what others deal with and also encourage you to keep your eyes open for signs of people in your life going through such situations. You will never know how much your help would mean to them. If my story can help at least one person in any way, then I feel that my purpose will be fulfilled.

There is always a light at the end of the tunnel—if you want there to be one. If you have a similar story or are carrying any form of pain you can't seem to let go, please never give up on yourself. I won't lie to you; it will be a daily struggle to shake off the pain and effects your abuse has on you, but you can and will prevail.

The things that we are forced to go through don't define us; the way we respond does. I hate that I had to lose everything before I decided to start my healing process. It has been an exciting adventure, learning who I am as a person and finding myself. Don't wait too long to free yourself.

Thank you for allowing me the opportunity to tell you my story. My hope is that no matter what you are facing, this brought you some form of hope or strength for your future.

Don't let your abuse destroy you; let it be the fuel that inspires your success.

Many people facing abuse don't know who to turn to, so here is my e-mail address for anyone who would like to speak or reach out for help in any way.

Throughmyeyes973@gmail.com   DMH

www.ingramcontent.com/pod-product-compliance
Lightning Source LLC
Chambersburg PA
CBHW071449040426
42445CB00012BA/1492